THE ALHAMBRA

A t the base of the hill to the east is the Cerro del Sol (Hill of the Sun). Between the Alhambra and the Silla del Moro (Moor's Seat) and the Generalife is the valley called Aikaibia», now known as the Slope of the Death or of the Rey chico (Little King).

To the north of this triangle is the river Darro, the western end finishing at the Alcazaba and the south "Handaq as Sabika" (the Moat of Melted Silver).

The top of the hill where the Alhambra stands is more than seven hundred meters above the sea level and is an eroded formation of the Sierra Nevada mountains, formed of detritus shist and quartz. Although more recent than some of the formations, it was proper rock, and has by various crystallizations gained the required resistance and stability. If, to this stability, one adds rich ferrous materials in the soil, (reason for the red colour), one can understand why the hill has served as a firm, solid pedestal for the castle of the Alhambra for so many centuries.

Shaped like a boat, it's prow is formed by the Alcazaba pointing towards the city, with a length of over seven hundred meters from the Alcazaba to the tower of the Cabo de la Carrera and a beam of more than two hundred meters at its widest, giving an area of some thirteen hectares and having a perimeter of over two kilometers of walls and some thirty towers, some of them only ruins.

The very recent publication of the book "Foco de antigualuz sobre la Alhambra" (focus of ancient light over the Alhammbra) by Emilio García Gómez,(+1.995) using a text of ibn Al-jatib discovered in Rabat, ('Rooting through my saddlebags to entertain myself in my exile'), has caused all existing theories, solid or eccentric about the Alhambra, to be shaken as if by an earthquake until they collapse in a thousand pieces, and those held to be "profound studies of the Alhambra" by the the Sacred Cows of Arabism or Islamic Archeology, or simple studies of Arabic Art which have arisen in past

centuries, all are undone by the evidence of a contemporary of Yusef I or his son Muhammed V, the great builders of the Alhambra.

Firstly, with the new unitary view of the monument we have to throw out, at last, all the functional divisions of Mexuar, Serrallo, Harem, amongst which the Italian word "Serraglio (from the Turkish, via the Persian, meaning "harem" too) is seen as a separate dependency of the private dwelling of the king.

Another point to remember, and often forgotten, is what the Alhambra represents as architecture: this has always been undervalued. We all become tourists when faced with the monument. In the "Manifiesto de la Alhambra" prepared by a group of Spanish architects in 1953, it says 'The Alhambra has never been looked at from the architect's point of view: strangely, even architects faced with the Escorial sharpen their professional eye, when they arrive at the Alhambra, slacken their perspicacity and become mere curious tourists: even to the extent of excusing their complacency by recourse to their emotions: "Yes, I like this, but not as architecture".

Later on the same text they add: "The relationship between this XlV'th century and the most progressive modern architecture is, in some points, astonishing: the human scale is seen in both, the use of organic asymetry in the composition of levels, the way the garden and landscape are related to the building form, the strict economic use of materials, without frills, and in many other ways too numerous to mention".

Thus, the Alhambra, despite its great age, is in concept and construction an architectural complex of great modernity. To quote a modern architect of recognized prestige, the Swiss architect Le Corbusier found in the monument his definition of modem architecture: the intelligent interplay of volumes correctly and magnificently united under the light, an idea established in his "Cité Modeme" (1922). In his buildings he attempts to bring garden and landscape into interiors, and he always uses the human scale as his module.

In the Alhambra, the harmony of asymmetry, the contrast of light and shade, light reducing mass, the focus of sky in the building, water and landscape, the mast and lintel structure, "the agile use of nature in the planning of buildings" are some of the architectural solutions which add to the modernity.

Prieto Moreno, to whom these last words belong, and who was for many years the Architect Conserver of the Alhambra, apos."*the Alhambra combines in its buildings many architectural concepts which are still valid today, and, of course, they are considered masterpieces*". Another

achievement in the construction is the way that the perpendicular axis of the courts is mantained, given the irregularity of the site and the different ages of building. This gives the impression of a regular and harmonic whole.

Francisco Pi y Margall assures us, that the Alhambra 'grew century by century, and every day increased in splendour»'. In effect, the Alhambra was not planned from the beginning as a union of various constructions, rather it grew from the citadel which existed at the end of the IXh century. This sufficed, (in 1238), as the residence of Muhammad ben Yusef ben Nasr, lord of Arjona. When the kingdom of Granada began to grow in importance, that citadel was not sufficient for a real king: starting with the old castle Nasr and mosques, schools, etc. until it became a palatial city capable of housing an increasing and aristocratic population.

At the end of the reign of Muhammad ben Nasr -who helped Fernando III in the conquest of Seville in1248- there was a period of peace based on a truce with the Castillians. At the same time diplomatic and administrative needs increased in a kingdom which covered a territory from Gibraltar to the frontier with Murcia, joined to the sea by a coastal line from ancient Calpe to the river Almanzora, and including the provinces of Granada,

Almería and Málaga, with parts of Jaén, Córdoba, Seville and Cádiz, a long frontier marked by a number of towns still called "de la Frontera".

A century later, during the reigns of the great builders Yusuf I and his son Muhammad V—especially at the end of the later reign—the Alhambra, seen from the Albayzín, was a white castle on a plinth of vegetation reaching down to the nver Darro. This forest which served as a zoological garden where the animals ran free, was viewed from the innumerable windows of the palace. From the farms and country houses of the Vega (plain), then a forest of fruit groves, which concealed a population almost equal to that of the city (according to Andrea Navaggiero), the Alhambra stood out white and brilliant in the setting sun like a flash of golden light on the terraced gardens of the Generalife and Cerro del Sol and at its far background Yabal Sulayr (the Mountain of the Sun and Snow, Sierra Nevada) framed by the blue sky.

But, if the Alhambra was white, why was it called "La Roja", (the Red)? We venture a personal hypothesis, that the name «Hamra» (The red) was given as an analogy of the family name of the founder of the dynasty, al Ahmar, that is "The Red", and this name became common place in the XIV'th century.

The white rendering can clearly be seen on those walls and towers which have not suffered major restoration, conserved areas, large or small, of the onginal finish.

Finally, we draw attention to the use of the name Moslem instead of Arab when speaking of the ancient inhabitants of the Madina al-Hamra'. Arab relates to a certain extent a nationality, and the creators of this Medieval Wonder were Spanish, grand-children and great grand children of Spaniards, who spoke Arabic and practiced Islam; the product of a happy fusion of races who were the founders of a culture which has no equal.

To present this book to the reader we recall the words of F. Villaespesa, from Almería, dedicated to the Alhambra, and which may be seen on a plaque near the Puerta de las Granadas:

Though not even a shadow of the walls remain,
the memory of the place is eternal,
a unique refuge for dreams and artistry.
Then the last nightingale, which breathes upon the Earth
will come to build his nest and sing his songs,
like a last farewell,
amongst the glorious ruins of the Alhambra.

THE GATE OF JUSTICE

Today this is almost the only entrance to the walled enclosure of the Madina Al-Hamra (The City of the Alhambra). It is a square shaped tower joined on one side to the wall which enclosed the aristocratic city known today as the Alhambra, and it is without any doubt, the most important doorway to the monument.

A spandrel of white marble decorated with plaques and strapwork painted green sits above the segmented lintel over the inner arch, where one can see a symbolic key , and below a copy of a gothic Virgin Mary, one can see in a beautiful inscribed panel of arabesque characters: "This Gate called bab al-sari'a was ordered to be put up, may God make the justice of islam prosper and be a sign of His glory for a long time, by the Emir of the Moslems, the warrior

Sultan and Just, Abu-l-Hayyay-Yusuf [...]". This work was completed in the month of the Glorious Nativity of the year 749" That is June 1348, the same year that Giovanni Bocaccio wrote his "Decameron" while isolated in a country villa to escape the terrible "Black Death" which swept Europe and which shortly, like an apocalyptic blow, would reach our peninsula as the "The Great Slaughter" causing massive loss of life in Andalucía.

The name Gate of Justice could be supported by the part of the inscription which says "May God make the justice of Islam prosper within her". As to the name 'Gate of the Esplanade', this refers to the existence of an esplanade prior to the building of the roads to the Generalife and the forest.

The open hand incised on the key-stone of this first arch has given rise to many theories as to its significance. At first, and long ago, the open hand with the palm forward was a sign of peace: it is the natural posture at the approach of an enraged rival. But, in this case, it seems that the significance is in the five fingers, which the Muslims call al-Hamza (the five), that is the five fundamental precepts of Islam: believe in one God, prayer, alms giving, fasting and the pilgrimage to Mecca.

At the level of the roof terrace there are two gargoyles, that in times of war could support a gallery or barbican and in this way covered any blind angles around the tower.

Behind this outer arch, due to its massive size never had any doors, is a separation or defensive wall- typical of the innovative nazarite military architecture-, for hurling down boiling oil or molten lead from above.

This second arch, made of marble, as is the whole archway, was probably polychromed in the Hispano-Musulman period. It is decorated with a shell above the keystone, and another two at the same height at the edge of the spandrels. The arch is decorated with vaussoir, alternately raised, resting on columns with cubic capitals and koranic inscriptions. At the center of the arch, on the key-stone, one sees a key with tassels. This has given rise, like the hand itself, to numerous theories; Hurtado de Mendoza, according Gallego y Burín, opined that this was the emblem of the kings of Granada. One can, of course, see this key and tassel over the nearby "Wine Gate" and over the entrance to the Generalife from the lower gardens.

Beyond this doorway is a horse-shoe arch of dressed stone on half columns, carved into the frame, with cubic capitals. Between the two arches are hung the iron cladgates, which retain their original lock and bolts. We enter under these arches into the access corridor of four right-angle turns in the Almohade style, covered by squinched vaults. These are much in keeping with the military character of the entrance, each turn becoming a point of defence.

On the wall opposite the exit, in one of the niches used as a bench for the guards in olden times, in 1588 the residents of the Alhambra set up an altar for the veterans of the garrison. However, the cisterns were built in 1494. The plaque must have been set up some years later and been nearer to the cisterns mentioned.

Very curious is the confusion as to the name of the Moorish monarch reigning at the time of the surrender, more so given the proximity to the event.

We finally emerge through the rear archway, discovered by Rafael Contreras in 1588. The outer face of this arch still preserves in its spandrels remains of mosaic, similar to those on the inner arch with the niche of the Virgin. They rest on a two centred arch of typical Hispano-Musulman style, and are decorated with a blind tracery of much restored bricks. The infilling of the rhomboids is different to that of the outer gate. To the north side of the gate is an inner moat, which extended all round the walls of the Alhambra at times covered, at others open, but always deep enough to allow cavalry patrols.

The opposite wall, with one's back to the gate, has a rampart which runs from the top of the tower. This wall which seems to have collapsed in the early XVIth. Century was rebuilt with grave stones; possibly from the nearby cemetry of Maqabir al-Assal. or, perhaps, from the Yabbanat Bab-al Fajjarin (Potters Gate Cemetery) which according to Ibn Aljatib *"was placed next to the governor's residence"*, that is the royal cemetry of al-Fajjarin to the south of the Alhambra above the Jewish quarter of Mauror near Torres Bermejas.

These stones are poor material, rough hewn with inscriptions of cufic characters at the edges. Their poor state contrasts with the marble burial stones of the royal family, conserved in the Museo Hispano-Musulmán. Found in the Royal Rawda (cemetry), inside the Palace, coloured and gilded, they lead to the belief that the ones in the wall have a more humble origin.

THE ALCAZABA
(The Citadel).

The Alcazaba, unjustly forgotten by those who wrote about Granada after the conquest, blinded by the Alcazares of the Nazarite, is the embryo from which the aristocratic city (later called *Madina al-Hamrá*) was born.

During the civil wars of the IXth century and the battles against invading Almoravides and Almohades it was known under different names until after the XIIIth century the name Qa'lat al Hamra' (Red Castle) became common place the same as it carries to this day.

From the top of the Torre de la Vela (Watching Tower) one can clearly see two enclosures, one within the other. The smaller inner one is probably of Roman origin, as can be deduced from the foundations visible in the lower part of the walls, and Califal as it was rebuilt in 889 during the defense of this fortress against the Mozárabes and the Muladíes of Umar ben Hafsum.

Even after the arrival in Granada of Muhammad ben Nasr Al-Ahmar in 1238, the Alcazaba was for many years an isolated castle separated by a profound ditch from the area to the east, where the royal palaces were later to be built. During the time of Yusuf I a curtain of walls and towers rose over this, the remains of which can still be seen in the Plaza de los Aljibes (Water cisterns Court); one of these towers was used as a filter for the cisterns which the Conde de Tendilla ordered to be built in 1494, thus filling in the ditch.

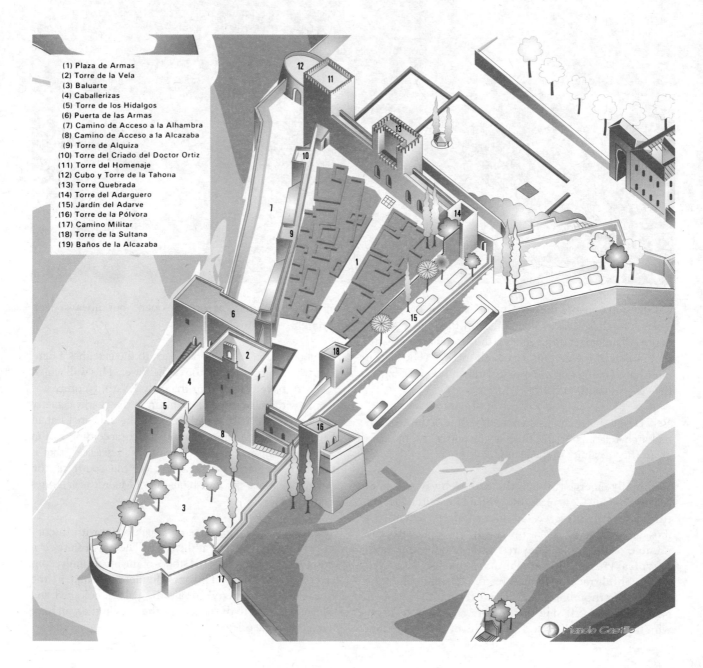

(1) Plaza de Armas
(2) Torre de la Vela
(3) Baluarte
(4) Caballerizas
(5) Torre de los Hidalgos
(6) Puerta de las Armas
(7) Camino de Acceso a la Alhambra
(8) Camino de Acceso a la Alcazaba
(9) Torre de Alquiza
(10) Torre del Criado del Doctor Ortiz
(11) Torre del Homenaje
(12) Cubo y Torre de la Tahona
(13) Torre Quebrada
(14) Torre del Adarguero
(15) Jardín del Adarve
(16) Torre de la Pólvora
(17) Camino Militar
(18) Torre de la Sultana
(19) Baños de la Alcazaba

King Yusuf I was also responsible for the joining of the royal palaces to the Alcazaba with a wall and inner passage, to which one ascended by a stair which still exists in theTower of Tahona (rediscovered in 1955 beneath the Cubo de la Alhambra), which is a renaissance construction, pot bellied and with no projection in order to reduce the effects of artillery fire, a weapon which was beginning to be useful at that time.

It would seem that Muhammad ben Nasr al-Ahmar was the builder of the Torre de la Vela at the western end. It has a height of twenty seven meters and a width of sixteen meters. It´s four stories have been much altered to adapt them as living space above all in the lower floor, thus the appearance of the interior is changed and the stairs have been moved.

The tower also lost some of its original height when the battlements were removed, generally due to the disasters it suffered since the XVI'th century: first an earthquake (1522), then the explosion of the power factory in the Darro Valley (1590) ·which left it in a sorry state·, and finally because a thunderbolt in 1882 which destroyed the belfry in its original position, the north corner of the tower.

The bell which was recast in 1773, replacing the original one, has the function of controlling the watering of the Vega. On more tragic occasions it called the city to be alert, as when the Alhambra caught fire in 1890.

The excellent view from the tower platform one can see to the north, the ancient district of the Albaicin, and to the east the gipsy quarter of the **Sacromonte** awaiting a promised restoration these last thirty years. Above this is the Hermitage of St. Michael which stands within the old walls of the city of Granada that "pour" into the valley, bearing the scars of centuries. The murmur of the Albaicín can be heard across the brutal roar of the traffic. In the spring time the Albaicin is enveloped by the perfume of flowers which when one is far from the city, still pervades in the memory.

All this is separated from the Alhambra by the **Valley of the Darro**, which extends to the right into the incredible **Valparaíso** (Paradise Valley) which has the perfume of fresh strawberries and the freshness of clean spring water. This is the Granada that Gautier described as "a celestial Jerusalem" and what Al-Saqundi, from Cordoba, described as "a pasture for the eyes and an elevation for the soul".

To the west spreads the modern city. To the south is the Hill of **Mauror** with the **Vermillion Towers**, a most ancient structure which protected the military camp there and the dungeons for the prisioners. To the left of this is the Carmen Rodríguez Acosta, modern, white and cold. Further to the left is the architectural cocktail of the Alhambra Palace Hotel and in the far distance, where the earth meets the sky, is the **Suspiro del Moro** (The Sigh of the Moor) and the last hillocks of the Sierra Nevada, its highest point to the south is covered by snow for most of the year; the

iron coloured foothills are peppered with romantically named villages. Nearer to the east side, stands the stony imperial architecture of **Charles V** and in the distance, at the foot of the Cerro del Sol (Hill of the Sun), stands the **Generalife,** the "garden without equal". There cypresses, like fingers of earth, thrust skywards begging for peace and silence for this landscape.

If one looks downwards, on the western side, one sees a military structure shaped like a Phrygian cap, its point turned towards the river Darro: this is the **Baluarte** (The Bulwark), a XVth century work made as a gun platform facing the city and is the real "prow" of the Alcalzaba.

The city of the Alhambra seems to have terrified the population of Granada more than any outside foe. This is the reason that, finding the citadel of the Albaicín encompassed by the surrounding suburbs and cutting of any escape to the countryside, the kings removed themselves to the Red Hill. Though this required major repair and construction, offered ample means of escape to the outside if flight became necessary, rather than at the western end: the Alhambra was entirely outside the enclosure of Granada.

On the south side, starting from the bulwark, runs the soldiers way which crosses the Bab Handac (The Ravine Gate) which was demolished in 1526 to build the Puerta de las Granadas (Pomegranates Gate). In the same period the Cuesta de Gomérez was opened up in order to give direct access from Plaza Nueva to the central road of what is now the forest of the Alhambra.

The wall continued down to Granada enclosing her within a spacious bailey defended by a number of castles and forts.

Before the building of the Puerta de las Granadas the entrance to the Alhambra began in the Plaza de Cuchilleros (Cutlers Square); zig-zagging through the districts of La Churra and Almanzora, one entered the fortified gate Bab Handac, and along the edge of the ravine of As-Sabika arrived at the Gate of Justice. Until the building of The Bulwark this urban way could have given access to the Alcazaba via a fork to an Almohade style doorway. Filled and uncovered again in 1857, this doorway can be seen near the south foot of the Torre de la Vela.

The **Puerta de las Armas** (Gate of Arms) which is the true main gateway to the Alcazaba, was equipped with a portcullis, its raising and lowering controlled from the floor immediately above the entrance. One reached there along the walled road of the Alcazaba: this tower is attached to the bailey of the Alcazaba and next to the Vela. The entrance to the Torre de la Armas is a wide passage which turns sharp right to meet a large space (certainly the guardroom) where the way opens in two directions: one to the left leading to the royal palace and the other to the right which gives entry to the Alcazaba.

The visitor to the royal residences (whether on horse back or on foot) was required to go some ninety meters with his right side exposed to the crossbowmen on the inner wall— the shield was borne on the left side—. Passing first a gate, since demolished, one came to the next point of control at the Torre de la Tahona and then to a market or zoco (its remains can still be seen) which was held by tradition in the entrance of all fortified cities.

At the end of a pebble paved slope our visitor arrived in the Plaza de las Armas. Before his gaze was now a central street with a bath house for the soldiers to his left. On both sides were houses for the officers of the garrison, armorers, blacksmiths etc, the foundations of which are still to be seen. There are also water cisterns, ovens and a dungeon.

This Plaza de las Armas is enclosed by the following towers, starting from the Torre de la Vela: **Torre and Puerta de las Armas, Alquiza, El Criado del Dr. Ortiz** (The servant of Dr. Ortiz), and in the north west corner, la **Torre del Homenaje** (The Donjon), similar in height to the Torre de la Vela and irregular in plan (12.12 x 10.45 mts.). Its five floors, including the cellars, served first as the residence for the wardens and then as a prison for Algerian pirates and francophiles.

The Torre del Homenaje is one of the oldest in the Alcazaba, dating from the period of the Caliphate. An archaeological study of the materials of which it is constructed compared with those at its base, leads one to think that perhaps Al-Ahmar ordered it to be rebuilt on the ruins of a tower dating from the ninth century.After the Torre del Homenaje comes the **Torre Quebrada** (Cracked Tower) so called because of the long crack to be seen from the Plaza de los Aljibes, looking like a wound from head to toe. It is solid to the top of the wall, having two floors above this level.

Next comes the **Torre del Adarguero** (Leather-shield Maker) of which only the shell remains. To the right of the Torre del Adarguero is the former entrance to the Alcazaba which leads directly to the Jardín del Adarve. This garden is the old moat which divided the inner and outer baileys and was filled in with rubble and earth in the early XVIIth century by the Marqués de Mondéjar, to make the garden. The original moat depth can be imagined by observing the height of the cypresses planted at the foot of the outerwall.

On the inner wall there were two small towers, of which only the **Torre de la Sultana** remains. Through this garden going west, one reaches the **Torre de la Polvora** (GunpowderTower) which marks the start of the above mentioned Camino Militar to Torres Bermejas. From here, through another small tower, one enters the Torre de la Vela by a modern entrance at the level of the second floor.

From either the Adarve gardens or from the Torre de la Polvora the view is so spectacular that any description can only diminish it.

La Alcazaba — The Fortress — Citadelle — Die Festung — Rocca fortificata

Albaycín

ALHAMBRA

&

1.- ALCAZABA
2.- P. CARLOS V
3.- P. JUSTICIA
4.- PILAR CARLOS V
5.- F. MEXUAR
6.- T COMARES
7.- LINDARAJA
8.- LEONES
9.- PARTAL & T. DAMAS
10.- JARDINES BAJOS
11.- PATIO ACEQUIA
12.- PATIO SULTANA

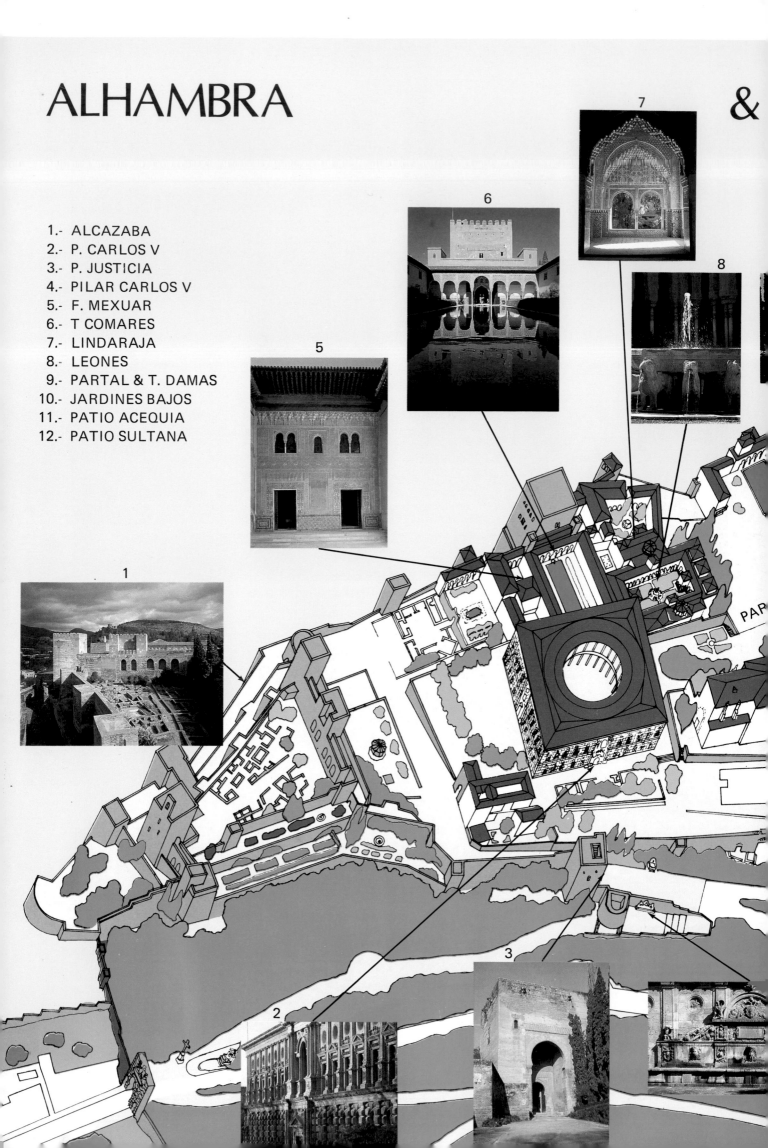

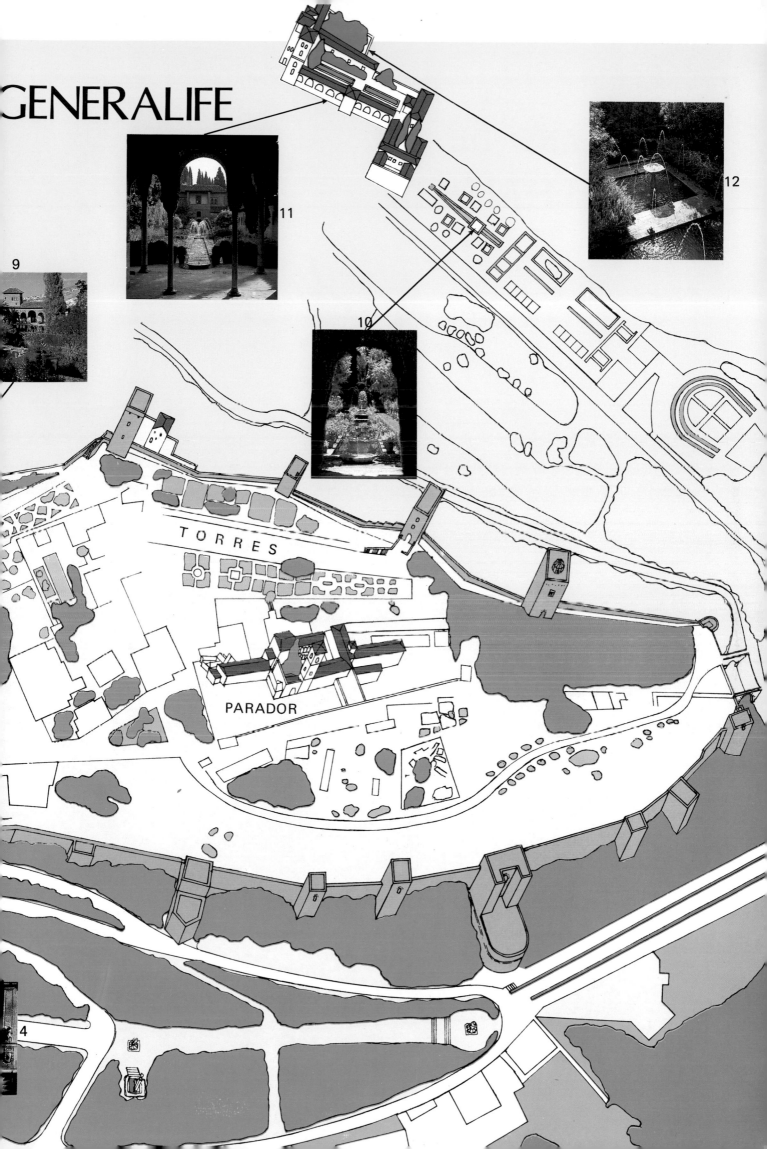

GENERALIFE

9

11

12

10

T O R R E S

PARADOR

4

PLANO DE
LA ALHAMBRA

Una deferencia de
Fábrica de Cervezas
La Alhambra, S. A.
Granada

EMPLAZAMIENTO

A Colina o Monte de la Assabica.
B Río Darro.
C Barrios del Albaicín y de la Alcazaba (antigua Iliberis) y Sacro-Monte.
D Valle de la Assabica (Barra de plata fundida).
E Monte Mauror (donde se levantan las Torres Bermejas).
F Cuesta del Rey Chico o de los Chinos.
G Cerro del Sol (asiento del Generalife).

En la Alhambra pueden distinguirse tres partes bien diferenciadas:

H Alcazaba.
I Palacio Real.
J Alhambra Alta o Población (Medina Alhambra).

0 10 20 30 40 50 60 70 80 90 100 m.

DOCUMENTACION TECNICA: Planos y maqueta de la Escuela de Arquitectura de Madrid.

ACC

1 Cuesta de los C
2 Puerta de los las Granadas, en das de la Alha el lugar que oc de los árabes (p nuevas).
3 Cruz de Leandr
4 Pilar.
5 Subida directa Pilar de Carlos
6 Pilar de Carlos
7 Puerta de la J planada, del Tr (entrada a la Alh
8-8 Subida a las To
8-9 » al Camp y Generalife (po
10 Subida (y bajad
11 Alhambra, Cam y Generalife.
12 Subida al Gener
13 Camino al Gene Rey Chico.

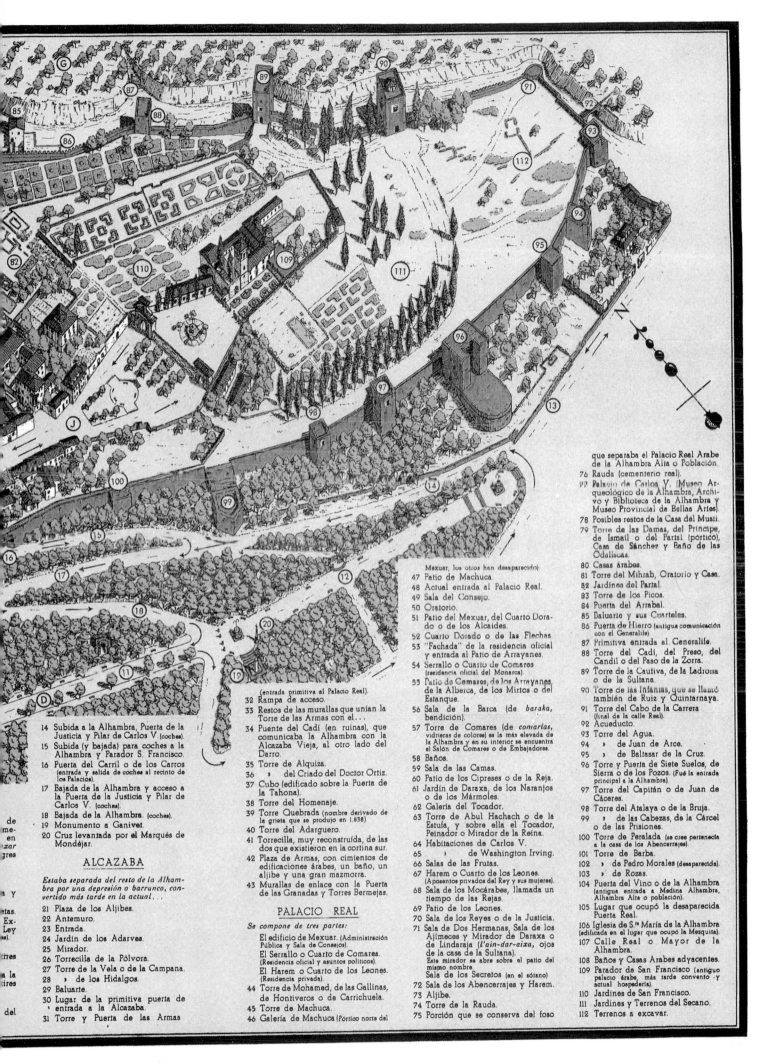

14 Subida a la Alhambra, Puerta de la Justicia y Pilar de Carlos V. (coches).
15 Subida (y bajada) para coches a la Alhambra y Parador S. Francisco.
16 Puerta del Carril o de los Carros (entrada y salida de coches al recinto de los Palacios).
17 Bajada de la Alhambra y acceso a la Puerta de la Justicia y Pilar de Carlos V. (coches).
18 Bajada de la Alhambra. (coches).
19 Monumento a Ganivet.
20 Cruz levantada por el Marqués de Mondéjar.

ALCAZABA

Estaba separada del resto de la Alhambra por una depresión o barranco, convertido más tarde en la actual...

21 Plaza de los Aljibes.
22 Antemuro.
23 Entrada.
24 Jardín de los Adarves.
25 Mirador.
26 Torrecilla de la Pólvora.
27 Torre de la Vela o de la Campana.
28 » de los Hidalgos.
29 Baluarte.
30 Lugar de la primitiva puerta de entrada a la Alcazaba.
31 Torre y Puerta de las Armas

32 Rampa de acceso.
33 Restos de las murallas que unían la Torre de las Armas con el...
34 Puente del Cadí (en ruinas), que comunicaba la Alhambra con la Alcazaba Vieja, al otro lado del Darro.
35 Torre de Alquiza.
36 » del Criado del Doctor Ortiz.
37 Cubo (edificado sobre la Puerta de la Tahona).
38 Torre del Homenaje.
39 Torre Quebrada (nombre derivado de la grieta que se produjo en 1.838).
40 Torre del Adarguero.
41 Torrecilla, muy reconstruida, de las dos que existieron en la cortina sur.
42 Plaza de Armas, con cimientos de edificaciones árabes, un baño, un aljibe y una gran mazmorra.
43 Murallas de enlace con la Puerta de las Granadas y Torres Bermejas.

PALACIO REAL

Se compone de tres partes:

El edificio de Mexuar. (Administración Pública y Sala de Consejos).
El Serrallo o Cuarto de Comares. (Residencia oficial y asuntos políticos).
El Harem o Cuarto de los Leones. (Residencia privada).

44 Torre de Mohamed, de las Gallinas, de Hontiveros o de Carrichuela.
45 Torre de Machuca.
46 Galería de Machuca (Pórtico norte del

Mexuar, los otros han desaparecido)
47 Patio de Machuca.
48 Actual entrada al Palacio Real.
49 Sala del Consejo.
50 Oratorio.
51 Patio del Mexuar, del Cuarto Dorado o de los Alcaides.
52 Cuarto Dorado o de las Flechas
53 "Fachada" de la residencia oficial y entrada al Patio de Arrayanes.
54 Serrallo o Cuarto de Comares (residencia oficial del Monarca).
55 Patio de Comares, de los Arrayanes, de la Alberca, de los Mirtos o del Estanque.
56 Sala de la Barca (de *baraka*, bendición).
57 Torre de Comares (de *comarías*, vidrieras de colores) es la más elevada de la Alhambra y en su interior se encuentra el Salón de Comares o de Embajadores.
58 Baños.
59 Sala de las Camas.
60 Patio de los Cipreses o de la Reja.
61 Jardín de Daraxa, de los Naranjos o de los Mármoles.
62 Galería del Tocador.
63 Torre de Abul Hachach o de la Estufa, y sobre ella el Tocador, Peinador o Mirador de la Reina.
64 Habitaciones de Carlos V.
65 » de Washington Irving.
66 Salas de las Frutas.
67 Harem o Cuarto de los Leones. (Aposentos privados del Rey y sus mujeres).
68 Sala de los Mocárabes, llamada un tiempo de las Rejas.
69 Patio de los Leones.
70 Sala de los Reyes o de la Justicia.
71 Sala de Dos Hermanas, Sala de los Ajimeces y Mirador de Daraxa o de Lindaraja (*l'ain-dar-aixa*, ojos de la casa de la Sultana). Este mirador se abre sobre el patio del mismo nombre.
Sala de los Secretos (en el sótano)
72 Sala de los Abencerrajes y Harem.
73 Aljibe.
74 Torre de la Rauda.
75 Porción que se conserva del foso

que separaba el Palacio Real Arabe de la Alhambra Alta o Población.
76 Rauda (cementerio real).
77 Palacio de Carlos V. (Museo Arqueológico de la Alhambra, Archivo y Biblioteca de la Alhambra y Museo Provincial de Bellas Artes).
78 Posibles restos de la Casa del Musti.
79 Torre de las Damas, del Príncipe, de Ismail o del Partal (pórtico), Casa de Sánchez y Baño de las Odaliscas.
80 Casas árabes.
81 Torre del Mihrab, Oratorio y Casa.
82 Jardines del Partal.
83 Torre de los Picos.
84 Puerta del Arrabal.
85 Baluarte y sus Cuarteles.
86 Puerta de Hierro (antigua comunicación con el Generalife).
87 Primitiva entrada al Generalife.
88 Torre del Cadí, del Preso, del Candil o del Paso de la Zorra.
89 Torre de la Cautiva, de la Ladrona o de la Sultana.
90 Torre de las Infantas, que se llamó también de Ruiz o Quintarnaya.
91 Torre del Cabo de la Carrera (final de la calle Real).
92 Acueducto.
93 Torre del Agua.
94 » de Juan de Arce.
95 » de Baltasar de la Cruz.
96 Torre y Puerta de Siete Suelos, de Sierra o de los Pozos. (Fué la entrada principal a la Alhambra).
97 Torre del Capitán o de Juan de Cáceres.
98 Torre del Atalaya o de la Bruja.
99 » de las Cabezas, de la Cárcel o de las Prisiones.
100 Torre de Peralada (se cree pertenecía a la casa de los Abencerrajes).
101 Torre de Barba.
102 » de Pedro Morales (desaparecida).
103 » de Rozas.
104 Puerta del Vino o de la Alhambra (antigua entrada a Medina Alhambra, Alhambra Alta o población).
105 Lugar que ocupó la desaparecida Puerta Real.
106 Iglesia de Sta María de la Alhambra (edificada en el lugar que ocupó la Mezquita).
107 Calle Real o Mayor de la Alhambra.
108 Baños y Casas Arabes adyacentes.
109 Parador de San Francisco (antiguo palacio árabe, más tarde convento y actual hospedería).
110 Jardines de San Francisco.
111 Jardines y Terrenos del Secano.
112 Terrenos a excavar.

Cervezas Alhambra para esta edición.

Bosque de la Alhambra — The forest — Le bois — Der Wald — Il bosco

Puerta del vino — The Gate of wine — La porte du vin — Weintor — Porta del vino

Oratorio y Albaycín — View on the Albaycín — Vue sur l'Albaycin — Aussicht über den Albaycin — Moschea e l'Albaycin

Mexuar

Fachada de Comares — Façade of comares — Façade de Comares — Hauptfassade von Comares

Patio de los Arrayanes

PLANO DE VISITA A LA ALHAMBRA Y EL GENERALIFE

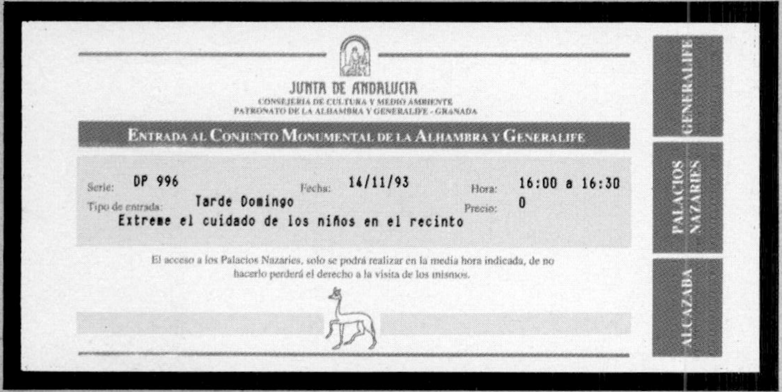

GENERAL

PALACIOS

ALCAZABA

CUESTA

TORRE DE LA CAUTIVA

PARADOR DE SAN FRANCISCO

TORRE DE LOS PICOS

SANTA MARIA

CALLE REAL

TORRE DE LAS CABEZAS

PUERTA DE LOS CARROS

JARDINES DEL PARTAL

TORRE DE LAS DAMAS

PEINADOR DE LA REINA

TORRE DE COMAREX

CARLOS V

BILLETES

ENTRADA

PUERTA DE LA JUSTICIA

PUERTA DE LA VELA

PLAZA DE LOS ALJIBES

CUBO

TORRE DE LA VELA

BALUARTE

1- PRISION
2- TORRE DE LAS ARMAS
3- TORRE DE LA VELA
4- CUBO

5- MEXUAR
6- CUARTO DORADO
7- PATIO DEL MEXUAR
8- PATIO DE LOS ARRAYANES (MIRTOS)
9- SALA DE LA BARCA
10- TORRE DE COMARES (TRONO)

JUNTA DE ANDALUCIA
CONSEJERIA DE CULTURA Y MEDIO AMBIENTE
PATRONATO DE LA ALHAMBRA Y GENERALIFE - GRANADA.

Entrada al Conjunto Monumental de la Alhambra y Generalife

Serie: DP 996   Fecha: 14/11/93   Hora: 16:00 a 16:30
Tipo de entrada: Tarde Domingo   Precio: 0

Extreme el cuidado de los niños en el recinto

El acceso a los Palacios Nazaries, sólo se podrá realizar en la media hora indicada, de no
hacerlo perderá el derecho a la visita de los mismos.

| GENERALIFE |
| PALACIOS NAZARIES |
| ALCAZABA |

PALACIOS

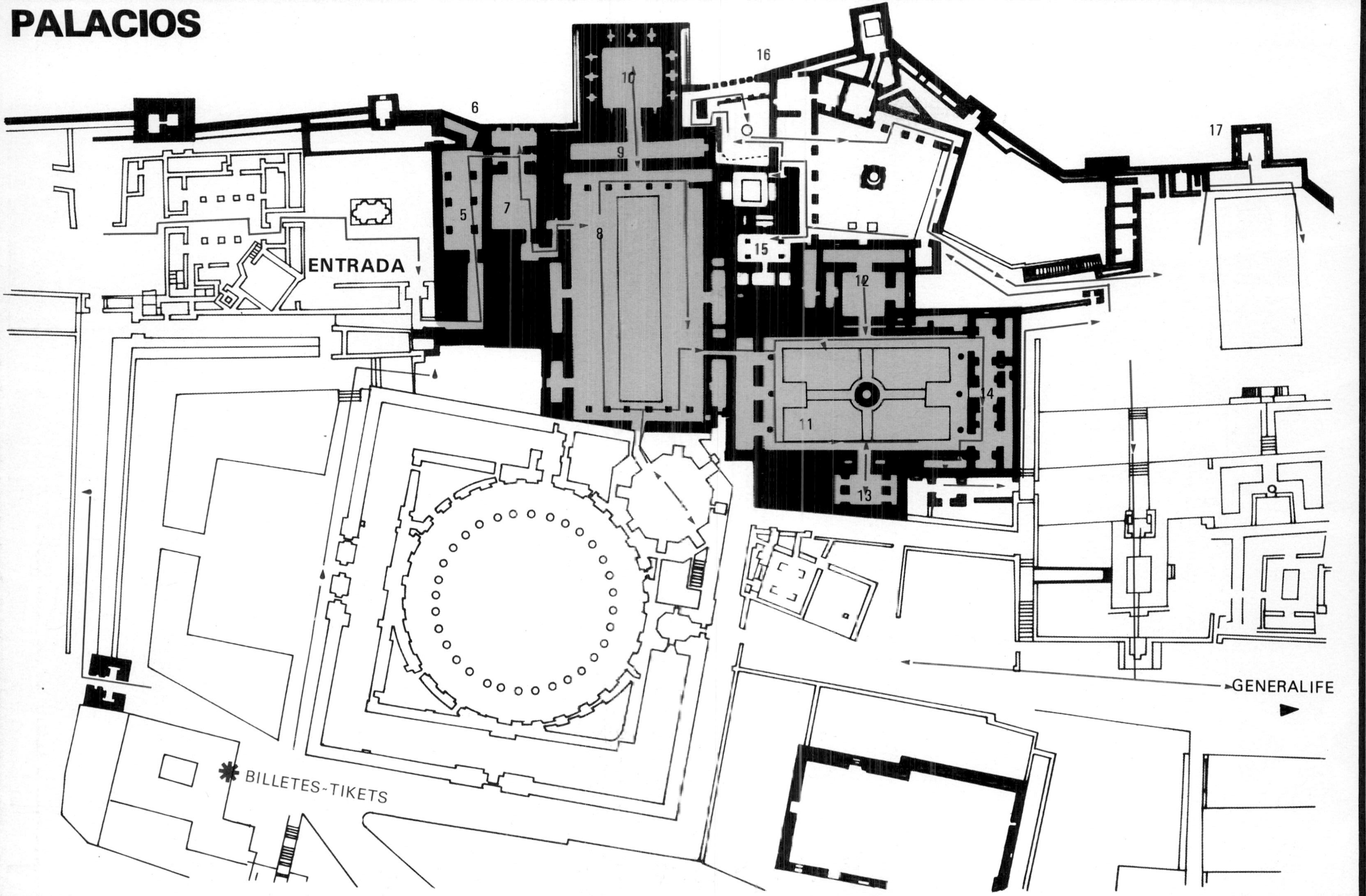

ENTRADA

BILLETES~TIKETS

GENERALIFE

5
6
7
8
9
10
11
12
13
15
16
17
4

ALCAZABA

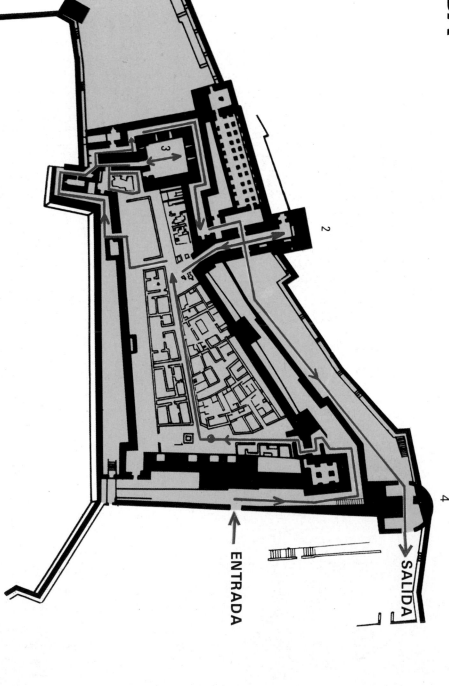

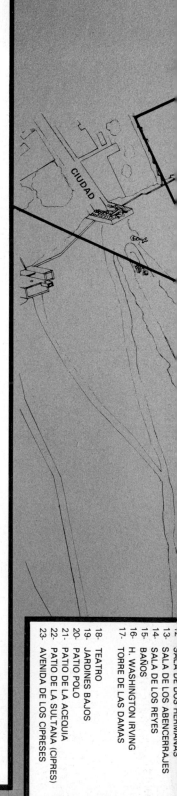

ENTRADA

SALIDA

2

4

3

CIUDAD

DISEÑO: J. MEDINA. TALLER DE
DISEÑO GRAFICO Y PUBLICACIONES

Edilux

Salón del trono — Hall of the ambassadors — Salon du trone — Thronsaal — Salone del trono

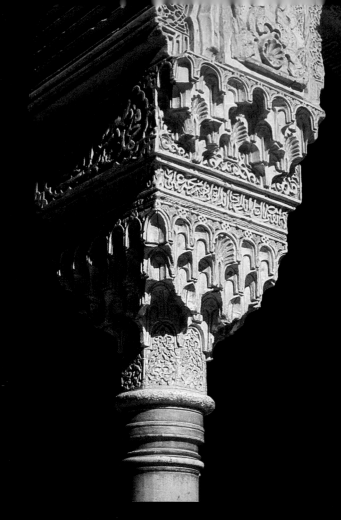

THE OLD ROYAL PALACE

THE HALL OR ROOM OF THE MEXUAR

This is the part of the palace which has suffered most from conversions, almost always at the instigation of the Christian Governors in the service of their King, adapting it to new uses and functions, drastically altering the original appearance. These changes have meant the complete destruction of old structures, making it difficult to identify the original entrances to this part of the palace, where it seems the council met to decide important judical mattrers.

Those approaching from Granada, once they passed the filter of the Alcazaba and the control of the Tahona Tower, found themselves in a town square, or Zoco, a typical feature of town entrances (the Alhambra was a town). They then passed into a higher courtyard and finally they reached the Court of Machuca.

This court is so called because of the Machuca Tower on the side facing the River Darro, where the architect of the Palace of Charles V., and his son Luis (also an architect) lived. On the opposite side was a twin of this gallery but only some ruins on the floor remain. Its original form is recalled by some cypress arches.

The entrance to the buildings was very similar to the present one. A flight of ruined stairs at the end of the cypress gallery seems to confirm this. In the small upper court we find the entrance to the Hall of the Mexuar. This doorway, with its fine carved surrounds was, brought from some other location.

THE MEXUAR

This room, commonly called the Mexuar is probably the oldest part of the royal apartments to survive, even if it was much altered in the time of Yusuf I and his son Mohamed V. In a frieze of a what was a roof light at the centre of the room, one can read *"Glory to our lord Abul-Walid Ismail"*. This and its similarities to the Generalife, built and decorated by this King, leads to the belief that it was built in the early XIV'h century.

In plan there is a notable disproportion between the areas divided by the central columned area, the northern end, between the columns and the entrance being much the

larger. In this room a chapel was installed. As the room was found to be too small the end was demolished and a choir gallery built in the space gained with the pick.

In a recent excavation a small court with clay paviours was revealed under the choir gallery, proving that the room was enclosed at this side. The Mexuar was isolated from those whose business in the palace was not related to it.

The four columns at the centre of the room indicate the location of a roof lantern. It would have had clerestory lights on all four sides, filtering the daylight through coloured glass. Below this, in the square formed by the four columns, the Council met to decide important judicial matters. In the doorway there was a tile which said : *"Enter and fear not to ask for justice, for you will find it"*.

When the warden's residence (now the Hispano-Musulman Museum) was built above, the lantern was destroyed. The square space which remained, enclosed by the four columns, was covered with a radial wooden ceiling.

The west wall was thickened to take the extra weight, and the large, iron grilled windows which now light the room were opened in it.

The room was extended to include the small court. In the dividing line a choir Gallery was built, supported by a decorated beam resting on Arabic columns, with their bases sunk in the floor. To this was added a wooden railing and two more columns of the same style which reached the ceiling. The Moorish Oratory behind was used as a sacristy.

Despite all these viscisitudes the upper part of the walls of the hall conserve the original colour and gilding of the plaster decoration, and some of the wooden ceilings are original, recognisable by their polychroming and darker colour.

Above this work in ceramics (which lacks the brightness of the work it imitates), the length and breadth of the room we can read the litanies "The power of God", "The glory of God" and "The kingdom of God".

A plaster imperial crown can still be seen over the doorway, but the other one remains as it was on top of the column.

THE ORATORY OF THE MEXUAR

It was one of the parts of the Alhambra which suffered most damage from the explosion of 1590, so much so that it had to be completely rebuilt at the time, this work being completed in 1917.

On any plan of the Alhambra one can see that the Oratory does not follow the line of the walls; it angles sharply to the south east, seeking orientation towards Mecca for the Mihrab.

There are some inscriptions around the Mihrab, that says, *"Be not neglectful, come ye to pray"*,

THE COURT OF THE MEXUAR

This is a small court which, for no apparent reason, was called "The Court of The Mosque", in days gone by. On the north side is the Cuarto Dorado and opposite the impressive front which has been held until now to be the entrance to the Palace of Comares.

One has only to see the many engravings of this court made in the last century, to lose any reticence about the work of the restorer. In this case the restorations are numerous and well executed.

The court centres on a fluted, white marble fountain. This is a replica placed there in 1943 to fill the hole left by the removal in 1626 of the original one used as part of the Christian fountain in the Court of Lindaraja.

The demolition of a Morisco arch and the removal of the projecting floor which it supported has restored the former attractiveness of the Cuarto Dorado gallery. This gallery is composed of three well proportioned arches which rest on white marble capitals, possibly Almohade in origin. These in turn rest on slender white marble columns. The capitals are a stylised version, inspired by the zoomorphic capitals of Persepolis.

The Cuarto Dorado (Golden Room) beyond the gallery opens onto the woods through a Gothic window, divided by a mullion on whose head are the emblems of the Reyes Catolicos (Catholic Monarchs). The restoration dates from their reign and the original ceiling was preserved but redecorated with Gothic motifs. The ceiling rests on a frieze containing the emblems and motto of the royal couple.

On the eastern wall of the court is a tunnel which leads to the Baths of the Palace of Comares it has rooms on bothssides, once used as quarters for the guards and now used to store the results of the excavations being carried out in the Alhambra.

THE FAÇADE OF THE PALACE OF COMARES

To many authors this façade, on the south wall of the court, deduces the "existence of some architectural or decorative element in the court, to give the correct orientation". It is clear that this façade, intended as the entrance to the Palace of Comares, is far too monumental for this small dark courtyard .

A study of the manuscript by Ibn Aljatib, discovered in Rabat has lead don Emilio García Gómez to surmise that this façade, together with its doors, was originally sited on the southern side of the Patio de los Arrayanes and that it was the principal entrance to the Palace de Comares, but on the outside.

Later, through the records of building works in the Archivo de la Alhambra, he shows that in effect it was moved between 1537 and 1538 to its present location.

However, in Machuca's plan one sees two doors, which confirms Graber's hypothesis on the "existence of some architectural or decorative element to give the correct orientation".

The façade stands on a plinth of three marble steps and the moulded plaster decoration increases in complexity as it rises, perhaps in imitation of the classical orders. It finishes with finely carved, overhanging eaves, a fine work of carpentry, and rests on a frieze of the same material where decoration is no less perfect than the eaves or the rafters that support it.

This façade, much restored in the nineteenth century, has dividing strips between the decorative panels. There is an abundance of Magrebics characters surrounding the ajimez windows at the sides and a central window where we see repeated the dynastic motto:

"Only God is Victor".

In the frame around the doors, including the plaster jambs and the panel between the two, one can see various religious themes taken from the Koran written in cufic characters.

Above the lintels of the doors we can see the remains of the original tiling which has been continued in modern stucco down the jambs to the tile dado at the foot of the wall, also restored .

The aesthetic impression of this façade, wherever it was, must have been very moving: polychromed like a Persian carpet, with the mouldings and the eaves gilded, the polished bronze doors also looking like gold.

The right hand door leads to a post-conquest lobby, to some other Christian buildings and finally to the exit from the Arab palace. The left hand door leads to a small room with its ceiling and frieze gilded in the time of the CatholicMonarchs. Here in Gothic characters it erroneously says that Granada was conquered one year before it actually was (in 1492). At the end of its angled corridor we reach the Patio de los Arrayanes.

COMAREX

This complex containing the Hall of Ambassadors or the throne room is the most important of all the buildings in the Alhambra. The austerity of its design and the balance of its proportions fills the court with a serene majesty, so that one can breathe in the noble grandeur of the kings who built it.

The proportions are just perfect, so much so that when attempts are made to copy them on a smaller scale the effect is paltry, not to say ridiculous.

The Court of Myrtles was the centre of the diplomatic and political activity of the Alhambra, and probably the place of state reception for foreign ambassadors. It would be the place where important visitors would have awaited their turn to be received by the Sultan.

Until now the whole building has been attributed to Yusuf I. Despite the presence of a eulogy to Muhammad V on the north gallery celebrating his reconquest of Algeciras all the building works belongs to his father´s reign. However in Emilio Gómez's study of the aforementioned manuscript by Ibn Al-jatib it is made clear that the Court of Myrtles belongs to the period of Yusuf I.

It was in fact an open esplanade with a central pool. It was left to Muhammad V to enclose this esplanade, converting it into a monumental courtyard and preserving the northern buildings put up by his father, i. e. the gallery and Hall of the Ambassadors as well as the royal baths bellow the Palace.

The medieval visitor who entered from the south, having passed through the main entrance, found before himself a huge mirror of water reflecting the white mass of the Tower of Comares and, due to the slope of the white marble floors which permitted the water to reach the bases of the columns on the north side, these appeared to float on the water. All the buildings on this side including the tower became floating palaces. Thus when the rest of Europe was building "castles in Spain, in Granada they built palaces on the water". The most important function for the pool was that of a mirror, a feature used centuries later (1630-1647) in the well-known Taj Mahal in Agra (India).

If we suppose that the proponents of the theory about the entrance to The Hall of Comares are correct, the present entrance would have been a secondary entrance from the rooms in the Mexuar, never the solemn entrance to the residence of a king that one would expect.

On many occasions it has been stated that there were no tiled dados along the side walls but that there were some flower beds at their bases in which jasmin and roses grew. One only has to see the cut-away shape on the lower part of the door surrounds to see that there was a tiled dado at that level.

Richard Ford tells us that the daughters of Bucarelli tore down the ceramic tile surrounds that ran the entire length of the court and sold them off.

The south wall has a very recent ceramic dado copied from a sixteenth century one in the north gallery. This is a colonnade of seven arches covered by a seven domed ceiling of "lazo" (strap-work). At the east and west ends are another two takas, the western one being a modern reconstruction. The central arch of the gallery is higher than the others and rests on two capitals of Mocarabes in the style of Ispahan. Three others on each side are supported by cubic capitals.

Of the two doors which once existed on each side of the south wall only the one in the east corner with its plaster arch still stands, and leads by some stairs to the upper floor.

Behind the central arch is the so called "crypt of the Emperor's Palace". It is reached through the remains of a room severed diagonally by the stones of the renaissance palace. This room was similiar in its shape and size to the Sala dela Barca, although not so high.

The inside of the arch which leads to the crypt -of which we will write later- is adorned with foliate decoration in delicate tones of blue and above the arch are three windows with plaster jalousies. Above the roof of this gallery there is a long room which has seven windows opening onto the court (the central one, an Ajimez) and all have modern wooden jalousies. This long room which connects with the upper part of the Court of Lions was a concession to the women of the household, a form of discreet observation gallery from where they could watch the goings-on in the court without being seen.

There is a third floor above this last room. This is a seven arched gallery with a lazo ceiling. The central arch has a straight lintel, higher than the others and resting on

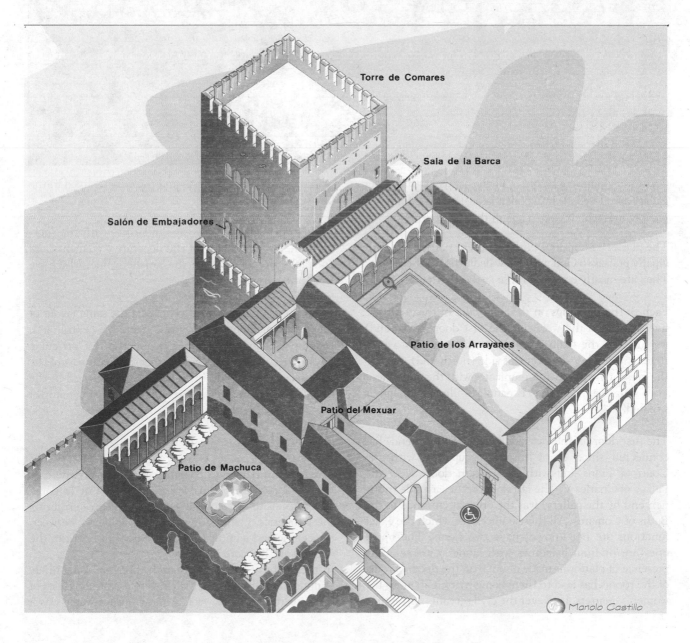

decorated hammer beams. All the voids of this upper gallery are closed off by wooden jalousies in the form of a parapet and which were made in the last century.

The plaster inscriptions of the southern portico are principally praises to God with a few dedicated to the Sultan. They are mostly copies of those at the north end.

Each of the buildings on the long sides of the court has five doors. On the west side the first door (south end) was used as the main entrance to the court for a long time, and the last door on this side (north end), next to the present entrance, communicates with the upper floor via a staircase where the Hispano-Musulman Museum is situated.

The first door on the east side (at the southern end) has connected since the Christian occupation with the Court of Lions and with the eastern doorway of the Palace of Charles V. The last door on the east side (northen end by the gallery) was the original entrance to the Baths of Comares. All these edifices, for which the exact functions are not known, have two floors. The upper ones are lit from balconies with ajimez windows. The presence of platforms made of brick on the floors of some of the rooms has lead to them being written about as the women's quarters. However the civil servants of the time worked sitting on low daises and the women lived in the Court of Lions.

The North Gallery has great similarities with the southern one because many of the decorative elements and epigraphs are copied from the northern one, which we shall now describe.

It has the same number of arches and the same layout of supporting members on capitals. The large central arch rests on Isphahan type capitals and the rest on cubic ones. The ceiling of this gallery together with part of the Sala dela Barca (Hall of the Boat) was destroyed in the fire of 1890 and masterfully rebuilt later reusing many of the surviving burnt pieces.

LA SALA DE LA BARCA

The greeting Baraka (a blessing) appears everywhere. It was the repetition of this word in the Sala de la Barca which seems to be responsible for its name by corrupting the phonetics. Considering also the similarity between the ceiling and a upturned boat, "barca" in Spanish, the name is all the more justified.

In the jambs of the entrance arch there are some finely sculptured marble niches which were used to hold jars of water, perfumes or flowers. Almost always water was a symbol of hospitality, as one gathers from the translation of the poem about the niches.

The gold coloured ceramics of the dado date this construction to the first half of the fourteenth century. The ceiling, a semicylindrical vault, was destroyed in the fire of 1890 but the present one which was built in 1965 compares favourably with the original.
The direct entrance to the Hall of the Ambassadors is under a large arch. Beyond this there are two narrow spaces.The lefthand one has a small door through which one can reach the different floors of the tower—these stairs offer a wide variety of vaulting on each landing and the right hand one is a small oratory where the Mihrab has been turned into a window giving light from the Patio de Lindaraja.

In the jambs of the next arch are two more small niches with verses in finely worked plaster giving clear reference to the water they contained, as on the right hand one where it says: *"The jar of water within me is like the faithful one in the quibla of the temple who remains absorbed in God… giving relief to those who thirst"*. In the left hand one it says: *"Whosoever comes to me thirsting I will lead him to a place where he will find clean water, cool, sweet and unpolluted"*. One can still see the remains of the gold leaf in the hollows of the mocarabes of this arch, and in the niches or takas are the remnants of the polychroming.

THE HALL OF THE AMBASSADORS:

Remain magnificent even though stripped of its stained glass windows which were lost in the explosion of 1590. This stained glass was a continuation of the design in ceramics on the dado, with the same geometry, where the fine lines interlaced in the ceramics were repeated in the lead fillets which held the coloured glass. The daylight was tinted by these colours and was cast onto the blue and gold floor tiles of which a few remain in the centre of the room, fenced off by chains.

Not all the tiles thus protected are original. The few that are, are the ones where the blue glaze and the royal shields they surround are smooth, not with raised edges between the colours to hurt the feet as in the more modern copies made after the reconquest and amongst which the originals are dispersed.

This room is a square of 11.30 metres each side, with three openings 2.50 metres deep on each side -this being the thickness of the walls of the tower- the centre window being an ajimez and the ceilings fine wooden "artesonados". The windows, which open to the north, east and west have two small windows above each. Almost at the cornice which supports the splendid ceiling there are five windows on all four sides which are reminiscent of

desert architecture. Those on the south side have been filled in as a means of reinforcing the wall against collapse. The central window ledge on the north side was the throne, according to the inscriptions on the wall above the tiling in this area where it says, "(...) Yusuf (...) chose me to be the seat of the kingdom. The lord of this kingdom makes it a great and divine throne".

From this position the Sultan exercised a certain psychological hold over the citizens of the capital who at the same time would have felt themselves under the gaze of the religious, political and military head of the kingdom.

From the moment they entered the doorway of the Sala de la Barca, the ambassadors would have felt intimidated by the silhouette of the Sultan seated against the light of the stained glass and looking upon them as they advanced across a sumptuous scenario of brilliant colours and sparkling gold.

Before the southern windows were filled in, the Sultan would have been able to sit or lie on his throne and simultaneously enjoy the view of the city with its gardens, and the reflections of the windows and sky on the water which lay before his eyes in the Court of Myrtles.

The ceiling is the masterpiece of the carpenters of the kingdom. It rests on a cornice of painted wooden "mocarabes" where one can read the Sura LYVII of the Koran or the Kingdom. In the third Aleya it says, *"He did make seven heavens one above the other; no discord will you see in this pious creation"*.

This is a clear reference to the seven heavens spoken of in the Koran in three of its suras , surely referring to the design on the ceiling of the room.This is made up of 8,017 pieces of wood with superimposed reliefs in cedar and made into various symmetrical panelsframed in a boss of mocarabes at the top of the dome.

Don Darío Cabanelas found a plaque showing the colours to be applied to this ceiling, white, red, walnut-white, light green, red, green and once again red in that order.

Amongst all the cufic, magrebie and hispano-cursive characters which include religious themes, the constant repetition of the device "Only God is the Victor" and the praises to Yusuf I (and one must be impressed by the decorative value of the Arabic epigraphy) and just visible on the capital of one of the niche arches, is a text indicating the public nature of the hall. Begging brevity, it says:

"Few words and you will leave in peace"

Sala de Dos Hermanas — Hall of the two Sisters — Salle de Deux Soeurs — Raum der Zwei Schwestern — Salla delle due Sorelle.

Patio de los Leones: Detalle — Detail — Détail — Detail — Particolare

Partal

Baños

Baths

Les Bains

Die Bäder

Bagno

←

Torre de las Infantas

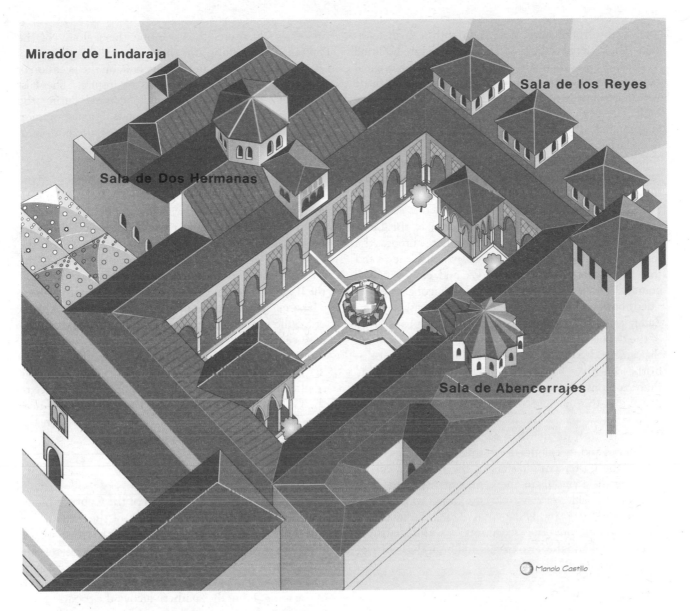

Mirador de Lindaraja

Sala de los Reyes

Sala de Dos Hermanas

Sala de Abencerrajes

Manolo Castillo

THE COURT OF LIONS

This was the centre of the Sultan's household and included the area given to the women of the royal house. It cannot be called harem for its function was not exclusively feminine in nature, as it was also used for activities related to diplomatic and political life of the kingdom.

We know now that on the 30th December 1362 the Court of Lions consisted of no more than the Hall of the Two Sisters and the buildings that now enclose it were erected after this date. The entrance was through a small door in the southern corner of the court and it leads into a small lobby which still contains remains of fine foliate decoration and benches for the guards.

As you passed through the entrance to the Court of

Lions, its beauty unfolded again little by little whichever of the two paths the colonnaded cloister directed you. A forest of golden columns opened up before the visitor and, continuing slowly along, resembled "*the golden fringes of a spread of lace suspended from the sky*", because the garden plants in the middle prevented you from seeing how the pillars rested on their marble bases.

The uniformity of capitals and arches is only illusory since there is great decorative diversity which is not apparent at first. The shafts of the columns are joined to the bases and capitals by lead joints so that reasonable thermal movement can be accommodated and a perfect assembly could be achieved for the three elements.

The shorter two sides of the court are not symmetrical either. On the east side on each flank of the prominent pavilion the columns stand in two pairs and a single one, whereas on the opposite side are two single columns and one pair on each flank. On the east and west sides of the court are two pavilions which intrude into the quadrilateral, each with a small fountain. The coffered ceilings of these pavilions are beautiful wooden domes which still conserve some of the original polychroming. These are two perfect hemispheres made with flat components. The western pavilion has its roof built above the original cornice and the intervening space is decorated with imperial eagles in plaster, recalling the period when its height was altered. This change in height is not entirely capricious, but a consequence of the difference in the line of sight between a man seated on the floor or lying down and another man standing up.

In the centre of the court the Fountain of the Lions sprays water and refreshes the atmosphere through the mouths of twelve white marble lions, which as they stand in a circle watch over every hook and cranny of the court. On their backs they carry a dodecagonal (twelve-sided) bowl and on its sides one can read a qasida by Ibn Zamrak which apart from being beautiful, explains many of the details of the court and of the fountain. Are these the same gilded copper lions which Ibn Aljatib saw before the court was built? The theory nevertheless exists that the lions were once polychromed and there is evidence that they have been scraped.

This court with its arches of perforated tracery forming rhombuses and its colonnades of fine pillars seems inspired by the Cistercian cloisters of the period, a theory aided by the fountain in the centre of the court. The rooms at the sides of the court are joined to the Lions Fountain by a sort of marble cross. Along its canals the water flows from the fountains to the halls of Abencerrajes and the Two Sisters and from the centre of the two pavilions.

THE HALL OF THE MOCARABES

This is the first room as one enters from the Court of Myrtles and the nearest to the original entrance. The name mocárabes means kinds of prefabricated plaster pieces which made up the vaulting. Wrecked in the explosion of 1590 this was replaced by a baroque ceiling of plaster. In the last century the southern end of the vault was taken down revealing the remains of the original, where one can see some of the polychroming and the spring of earlier work.

THE HALL OF THE ABENCERRAJES

We find this to the right as we pass anticlockwise through the colonnade. It is said that in Granada, myth and history are so intermixed that at times it is difficult to determine where one begins and the other ends. The name Abencerrajes belongs to a family of Granada of great political importance. Their rivals, the Zenetes, formed a conspiracy which implicated the Sultana in an amorous adventure, thus exciting the jealousy of the Sultan and leading to the massacre of thirty six Abencerrajes knights in this very hall, on the occasion of a party. This legend which was to inspire "The Last Abencerraje" by Chateaubriand, occurred during the reigns of a number of kings of Granada. Popular opinion has it that the red marks -iron oxide- on the bottom of the pool are the blood of the murdered knights.

This dodecagonal fountain is the central piece of the room, when filled and calm it reflects the magnificent mocarabes of the ceiling, with and eight-pointed star in the vaulting. From a seated position behind the fountain, before the Lions Fountain had the present spout, the view was a series of brilliant reflective planes and, at the far end through the Mirador of Lindaraja in the Hall of the Two Sisters one could see the old city and the sky. The original tiles in this room were taken to the Alcazar of Seville and replaced by the present ones in the sixteenth century.

In the south-east corner of the court is another exit leading to the gardens of the Partal and passing through a shell-domed tower. This is obviously another entrance to the Court of Lions coming from the Arrabal Gate near the Torre de los Picos which communicated with the approach road to the Generalife.

THE HALL OF KINGS

This occupies the whole east end of the Court of Lions. It is divided into five spaces; three of them lit by the access porticoes and separated by another two in the shade. In the springs of the vaulting of mocarabes there are twenty windows with plaster lattices. At the extreme ends are two alcoves with arches aligned along the axis of the room. From the southern alcove the rooms appear as a succession of areas of light and shade framed by plaster arches each different from the other.

This variety of decoration and alternating lights and shades results in this heavy decoration being pleasant to the eye without tiring in the way baroque decorative elements do when repeated over and again. The sensation of harmony with different elements is achieved in the ideal formula of modern decorators.

On the ceilings of the bigger alcoves there are paintings on vellum fixed to their wooden backing with paste and tiny bamboo pegs. This fixing system avoided damage which the rusting of iron nails would produce, and at the same time prevented the paintings from falling as the nails fixed in the wood loosened because of the differential thermal movement of the materials.

Veritable rivers of ink have been spent about the meaning of these paintings. Nowadays, however, there is little opposition to the demonstrated assertion of the French arabist Massignon. He destroyed the false argument which denies the eastern origin of these paintings founded on a supposed Koranic prohibition of representing living beings. The paintings of the Kings Hall are Moslem, even if influenced by western models, and it is generally believed that they were made in the late fourteenth or early fifteenth century. In fact in the Sura V, Aleya 92, the sacred book of the Mohammedan says: *"Oh, all those who believe! Verily, wine and the anzab, and the maisir and arrows (are) abominations and works by Shaitan; avoid them and probably you would be happy".*

Thus all that is forbidden in relation to living beings are the anzab or idols which can be objects of adoration. This limitation is not exclusive to Islam; worshipping of idols is also prohibited in the Old Testament and in the Talmud. Also there are so many examples of living beings in Islamic art that just counting them would give the lie to this pretended prohibition.

The central alcove, given its privileged position, would have housed the Sultan and his intimates. Seated within, the perspective is of an oasis seen through a forest of palm trees with the Fountain of Lions at its centre. On the ceiling of this alcove ten persons are also painted who are traditionally thought to be the first ten kings of the dynasty. The silhouettes of hands and faces and the stars which divide the composition horizontally into two halves are painted on a golden background, all being reminiscent of early Byzantine panels.

The paintings in the other two alcoves share certain thematic elements. Two personages, one Christian and one Moslem, to judge by their arms and dress, perform a series of tests and trials, apparently for the favour of a Christian lady. All this terminates in the next alcove where the Moslem defeats his rival with a lance thrust before the pleading Christian dame who watches the trial from a tower.

THE HALL OF THE TWO SISTERS

Contrary to earlier opinion this is now recognised as the oldest of the rooms around the Court of Lions. As with all the other adjuncts of this court where we do not know the original name, the one given is merely descriptive. It is called **The Two Sisters** because of the two large Macael marble slabs in the centre of the room.

This room was used as the Hall of the Ambassadors by Muhammad V and replaced that built by his father for the same purpose in the Tower of Comares. It is decorated with a tiled dado decorated with the family coat of arms and metallic glazes, perhaps the most unusual in the whole of the Alhambra. Above this dado, written in Spanish cursive characters, is a beautiful qasida by Ibn Zamrak which covers the four walls. Starting from the left (facing the Fountain of the Lions) it describes the beauty of the room, comparing it to a beautiful garden. It also speaks of the marvellous vault of mocarabes which cover the room, a real masterpiece of over five thousand pieces.

The square floor of the eight-by-eight-metres room changes to an octagon in the upper part by means of squinches of mocarabes which support the eight-sided ceiling. Two windows are placed in each plane of the octagon and until 1590 they projected coloured light through stained glass. The aesthetic effect of the room is captured in a verse of the afore-mentioned qasida, in which it says:

"… in this the soul will find a beauteous dream"

Entering this hall from the Court of Lions we can see two narrow passages to left and right, as in the Hall of the Abencerrajes. The right-hand one provides stairs to the first floor and the left gives access to a toilet.

The Hall of the Two Sisters is paved with great slabs of marble and at each side of a small fountain there are the two largest ones which give the room its name.

Passing through the Hall of the Ajimeces with its windows to left and right and with a ceiling of mocarabes we find ourselves in the fabulous Mirador of Lindaraja.

MIRADOR OF LINDARAJA

The name seems to be derived from the Arabic "ain-dar-Aixa" (the eye of Aixa's House). It is possible that once he had finished the Court of the Lions and what remained to be done of the Court of Myrtles, Muhammad V once again used the Hall of Ambasadors and designated the Hall of the Two Sisters for use by the Sultana (dar-al-Malika) and the royal family as a residence. This arrangement is described by Hernando de Baeza, former interpreter to the court of Boabdil and then secretary of the Catholic Monarchs.

This gazebo, with window ledges at the original height, has on its north side a bealltiful "ajimez" which overlooks the Garden of Lindaraja. Before the Christian gallery which encloses the garden was built one could see the city over the walls, and then turning towards the Court of Lions from a seated position on the floor one saw the sky through the window over the arch at the entrance to the Hall of the Two Sisters.

Horizontally one saw the fountain of this room and the mirror of water of the Fountain of Lions. Crowning this gazebo which once housed the throne is a stained glass dome held in the finest of wooden tracery. This filled the room with multicoloured lights in olden times. Around the ajimez of the gazebo is a poem from which we quote this fragment:

> "Certainly I am within this garden,
>   an eye filled with joy,
>   and the very apple of my eye is my Lord".

Could this poetic image of the eye have something to do with the provisional throne and the name of the gazebo?

All the dados here in are formed of very smallest tiles or cut ceramics and the jambs of the arch which separate the gazebo from the Hall of the Ajimeces have ceramic inscriptions in black which refer to Muhammad V; they are cursive arabic script and seem to be inlaid in a white background.

THE PALACE OF CHARLES V

In the history of art there can be no building more vilified than the palace commissioned by Charles V next to the Alhambra (the royal palace of the Mussulmans).

It must be understood that, although he was unbeaten in his European campaigns and Paladin of the wars against Protestantism, Charles does not get a good press in European history and that all he did and all that he ordered built is mercilessly criticised. The many great things that were done in his reign go blindly and completely unrecognised.

Even worse, our own historians with a few exceptions have imbibed from these polluted sources which come from abroad. Thus we see, to show but one example, that don Francisco Pi Margall, without pausing to meditate on the architectural marvel he had before him, let his pen write, "*is this but a mass of stones distributed by neither intelligence nor sentiment, or is it simply the drafting of compass and rule?*".

Don Luis Hurtado de Mendoza had succeeded his father don Inigo when, in April 1562, he had news of the coming of the Emperor Charles V to Granada after his marriage to Isabel of Portugal in Seville that March. Bermúdez de Pedraza, the historian, tells us that the emperor did not intend to visit Granada, but did so at the request of certain personages and not solely because of the heat in Seville. They sang the praises of the city which thirty years earlier had been the pearl of the kingdom. Owing to its exotic past it was very attractive to the young king who had passed his early years in the monotony of the Low Countries.

On the twentieth of April the majordomo of the emperor arrived in Granada to organise the reception of his monarch, and finally on the fifth of June, Charles arrived in the company of the fair Isabel, one of the most beautiful women of her generation.

Seven years earlier an obscure reredos painter called Pedro Machuca had arrived, accompanying Jacobo Florentino. They came from Italy where Machuca had spent some years —it is not known how many—frequenting Italian circles and, perhaps in the company of the Florentines, he came into contact with the leading figures of the Arte Nuovo. Its influence can be seen in the palace that was to immortalise him as an architect.

Despite Antonio de Palomino describing him as "a follower of Rafael", it seems that Machuca never reached the grade of Master Architect, and consequently his work was confined to the precincts of the Alhambra by special jurisdiction. He also counted on the patronage of Luis Hurtado de Mendoza, Count of Tendilla and Governor of the Alhambra, whom he had served as squire in 1526 and to whom he was probably bound by mutual affection. It is known that his oldest son and daughter were called Luisa and Luis in honour of his noble patron.

Once Charles and his followers had arrived in Granada they were installed in some rooms built the year before, next to the upper part of the Baths of Comares and around the Court of Lindaraja and had access to the rest of the palace through the Hall of the Two Sisters and the Hall of Ambassadors.

The rooms later occupied by Washington Irving in 1829 were built for Isabel of Portugal, and an extra floor was added to the tower of Abu-l-Hayyay which was to be known

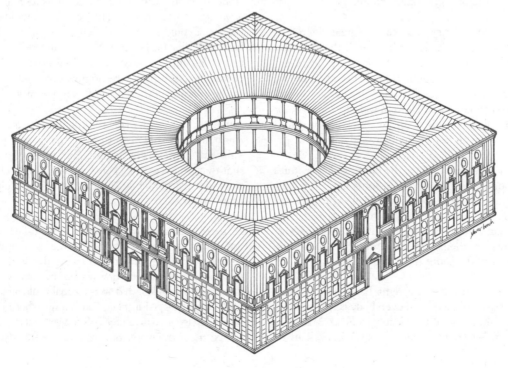

as the "Peinador de la Reina". The court was housed in different parts of the city and the Queen, after moving her lodgings to the warden's apartments above the Mexuar, finally decided to move to the Convent of the Jeronimas which had recently been built. Until December when the royal couple left the city, this was the heart and brain of the Empire. By that time the empress was carrying the future Phillip ll.

None of the more recent ancestors of Charles had had their own palace. With their evermoving courts they lodged in the houses of the nobility, in castles or monasteries.

Also, since the reign of the Catholic Monarchs and the early years of Charles' reign the colonial expansion looked towards Africa and the new lands of America. In the geopolitics of those times Granada had a privileged position as an inland city but not too far from the ports of embarkation for these continents. Because of his European education Charles could not live in the Nazari Palace, so he decided to build a palace on the Red Hill.

Pedro Machuca was commissioned to carry out the work with funds that Queen Juana of Castilla had destined, by order of her parents, for the repair of the old palaces, and 80,000 ducats which the emperor had received from the Moriscos of his kingdom.

The Morisco rebellion of 1568 put an end to the regular income to finance the works. After the 1550s the emperor's interest in his palace in the Alhambra was on the wane. Also his succesor, Philip II who was crowned king in 1556, was more interested in building the Escorial, leaving the Palace in the Alhambra in a secondary position. Successive delays, almost always due to a lack of funds, resulted in an unfinished palace up to the present day. It is considered to be the first non-religious renaissance building in Spain.

On the four exterior frontages one can see great differences between the two floors. The lower floor with the characteristic bugnato fiorentino (rustication), conserves the robustness of a medieval castle, while on the first floor (direct first by Luis Machuca and then by Juan de Orea) some "manerist" modifications by Juan de Herrera were introduced; for example, the illusion of walls of greater thickness produced by the round conical clerestory lights over the window.

On the western principal frontage the most notable features are the two winged, reclining women, softly carved in marble by the Flemish artist Antonio de Leval, which rest on the tympanum. He was also responsible for the cherubs above the tympana of the lateral doors, the medallions with Flemish warriors on them and the unfinished grey stone lions by the door of the south front.

Earl E. Rosenthal attributes the right hand relief (which represents the Battle of Pavia and everybody is left-handed) to this same Leval, though it is probably by Pedro Machuca. The left-hand relief (right-handed people) is by Juan de

Orea. All the other reliefs are allusions to the Triumph of Peace, with angels burning flags and the tools of war in the desire for disarmament.

The upper part of the facade is neither as rich nor as interesting. it gives the impression that the original design was simplified to the minimum possible. Here we truly see the "compass and ruler" which Pi y Margall spoke of. Two medallions by Ocampo of the trials of Hercules are the only sculptural features of note on this upper body of the facade.

The south front, on the other hand, has the two bodies of the facade in elegant harmony, although the reliefs by Nicolao di Corte do not have the strength of those on the main front. The other two fronts, to the north and east, lack any features of interest.

The thirty-metre diameter central court, reached by climbing a few steps, is the master work in this palace. The lower part of this monumental ring of thirty two Tuscan-Doric columns of a smooth pudding stone (porphyry), are reminiscent of Bramante's San Pietro in Montorio, as if it were cast from the same mould as that building but in negative and on a much larger scale.

The solution of the architrave detail is completely original, creating a perfect balance between the forces and resistance of the components of which it is made up. This ring rests on a torus (the curved vault of the gallery) which carries perfectly the outward thrust of the stones like a continuous flying buttress, one part resting on the outer walls and the other on the ring-beam. When this wall is weakened by an opening, as occurs on the west side, the extra load is carried by a lower vault or some other means of buttressing.

The upper level of the court, with ionic columns of the same stone as those on the ground floor, was roofed in 1967 with a wooden "Artesonado". The deep box-moulding and radical beams could easily have been the work of Pedro Machuca himself. The same occurs with the staircase in the south-east corner leading to the Museo de Bellas Artes. With its bold curves this far surpasses the original seventeenth century one in the opposite corner, despite its modernity.

Attempts have been made to find precedents for the plan of this building. It has been written that it was inspired by the Palace of Caprarola by Vignola, but it must be remembered that that palace with its pentagonal plan and circular court, was built in 1546 while Machuca's project is almost twenty years earlier.

A special mention must be made of the so-called "Crypt" which was mentioned in relation to the Patio de los Arrayanes. This is to be found under the unfinished chapel in the north-east corner of the renaissance court. It is now reached by a stairway in the vestibule on the east side. It has an octagonal vault, almost flat in section and star-shaped in plan, and has no other form of support other than its own curvature. This can without any doubt be considered one of the works of genius of the Renaissance.

THE GENERALIFE

Of the pleasure gardens on the Cerro del Sol, the Generalife is the only one to survive to the present day.

It was an estate where the King of Granada retired, away from the preocupations of the Court. Its proximity to the Alhambra (apart from the advantage of one being close to the centre of government and thus being able to attend to urgent matters during the holidays) was also a sign of the richness of the owner: when transport was by mule or on foot a recreational estate so near to one's permanent residence was an indication that the owner was very rich.

The opulence of the owner was in direct relation to the proximity of his country house.

The meaning of the name "Generalife" is obscured in utter confusion. Yannat al´arif, so says Ibn Aljatib, means "principal 'huerta' " (small holding or country garden), according to Seco de Lucena. "Huerta of the Architect" say other authors without realising that "ala-rife" is a term which takes in many activities, apart from the one they mention.

Are any of the architects of the Alhambra known? Since the designers of the palaces have been conspicuously ignored in the inscription in the palaces, it seems stran-ge to dedicate the most important gardens in Granada, if not the whole kingdom, to one of them.

Because of the shortness of this work we will have to leave aside the many versions of the origin of the name Generalife, but we cannot resist giving at least one of our "crop": the function of the Generalife is that of a "carmen" (Granada house in the city, with a garden) the residence where the people of Granada went in the autumn, the most beautiful season in this region. At that time the temperature is mild with neither the oppressive heat of summer nor the dry cold of winter. There are still flowers in the gardens, blue skies and little rain most days.

If we accept that the root "Yannat" is prominent in the majority of the theories, why not Yannat al-jarif or "the autumn garden"?

The Generalife was given by the Reyes Católicos to the 'comendador' (Warden) Hinestrosa. By a series of inheritances and marriages, etc. it came into the hands of the Granada Venegas family, thence finally to the Marqueses of Campotejar who were related to the Grimaldi-Palavicini from Milan. Following a long court case in which the State claimed ownership of the Generalife, the case was found in favour of the owners, who ceded the Palace to the Spanish State without cost, in 1921. For this act of generosity Alfonso XIII created the title of Marques del Generalife.

All that remains of the original gardens are the terraces where they were planted. These workings reached to the

top of the mount so that, from the top, one saw them as one entity down to the foot of the hill, with the variety of colours which the flowers and fruit trees imprinted on each of the steps. The present gardens have nothing in common with Medieval Gardens where flowers and fruits were mixed heterogeneously. In the present gardens only the senses of smell and sight are played upon. In the Mussulman garden one enjoyed the sight of the flowers, their perfume, the sound of water and the taste of the fruit eaten as one passed under the trees. This was a "huerta", a word difficult to translate into many languages, from the Latin 'hortus' and which was the common description of what today we call "jardín" or garden.

Any panoramic view from the Alhambra alone explains the reasons that promted its founder, the Al-Ahmar, to choose these hills for his palaces. They only lacked water to be perfect. The river Darro was diverted for 18 kms. to convert this wasteland into an oasis, the Paradise promised on Earth. Dams, channels, cisterns, siphons, ponds, right up to sand filters, all the mastery of Arab engineering, in short, was put to a human dimension.

Agriculture had been born in the East, the garden and the myth of the Earthly Paradise, idealized in the traditions and trnasmitted by the most ancient cultures which man has reported.

It would be difficult to imagine such irrigation in the Rhine, while the Euphrates, the Tigris and the Nile fertilize the deserts in this way. The Arabs, eager nomads and heirs of these traditions, mastered as no-one else, the physical laws that applied to water to confer the lifegiving force, symbolic of life, a subtle and mysterious nature that inpregnates these Gardens and Palaces with magic. Water was always the principal problem but also the first to be solved, to such a point, that its abundance determined the accessions during the successive invasions and re-population. Without water, neither Granada nor the Alhambra would be where they are.

To describe the Generalife, as it is known, it is necessary to refer to the Agriculture and Gardening treaty of Ibn Luyun, who listed the conditions, at the beginnung of the XIV century, that should to fulfil a property of this type:

"A small hill must be chosen to site a house among gardens so that it facilitates observation and guarding. The building should face south as too should the entrance to the property. The pond or well should be on higher ground, or better still, from the well, water channels run under the shades of the trees. All around there massive trees should be planted that are always green and all other kinds of plants that gladden the sight and, somewhat more separated, various varieties of flowers and other perrenial trees. A fence of vines should surround the garden and, in the center, the grapevines should shade the roads that straddle the paths.

A pavilion should be raised in the center for rest hours, surrounded by climbing rosebushes, myrtles and other varieties of flowers that beautify a garden. It should be long and wide so that it does not tire the eye while gazing upon it. In the lower part, a room should be built for the guests of the propietor. There should be a pond, hidden among the trees so that it cannot be seen from a distance. It is also convenient to build a dovecot and a small habitable tower, The house must have tow doors, so that remains more protected and it will be more restful for those that inhabit it."

All these conditions are found in what remains of the much-altered residence around the so called Patio de laAcequia (Court of the Canal or reservoir). The 'canal', which runs North-South along the spine of the court has, since the romantic period, two rows of spouts which, form water arches cascading into the canal in the Italianate manner. In this way the mirror effect which the pond had in the time of the Nazaries is broken and the air is filled with obsessive noise made as the fountains hit the surface of the water.

In the original design the water entered from the two fountains at the ends of the pool, forming a pleasant murmur, like calming music which does not interfere with one's thoughts.

In the time of the Reyes Catolicos some arches were opened in the western wall of the court, and its height was lowered. In the Islamic period there was only one opening in the wall, the pavillion at the middle.

The North end, the best preserved, is fronted by an arcade of round-headed arches. The centre one greater in height. These three arches of similar design are the entrance to a transverse space, covered with a wooden "lazo" ceiling. .The presence of a poem dates this building to the year 1319.

Translated by David H. Beaman

Edición y realización: Juan Agustín Núñez Guarde. EDILUX.
Fotografía: Miguel Román Vega y Juan Agustín Núñez.
Maquetación del texto: Germán Madinabeitia.
ISBN-84-87282-51-2 D.L. GR-1.925-89.
Encuardernación: Hnos Olmedo.

Texto: Aurelio Cid Acedo
Dibujos: Javier Bosch y José M. Medina.
Planos infográficos :Manuel Castillo
Impresión: Al sur, Copartgraf y Mateu Cromo.
Filmación: Francacolor.   Made in Spain

Generalife

Carlos V

Pags. 60-64: **Palacio de Carlos V, detalles** — Palace of Charles the V, details — Palace de Charles V, détailles — Palast von Karl V, Details — Palazzo di Carolo V, particolari